BORN Wild

in SHENANDOAH

Photography and text by
Ann and Rob Simpson

FARCOUNTRY
PRESS

Right: A white-tailed deer fawn nuzzles its mother's ear in Big Meadows, one of the best places in the park to see does and fawns in the spring and summer.

Title page: An eastern chipmunk perches on the branch of a box elder tree in Shenandoah National Park. Chipmunks are born in underground tunnels, where they remain for six weeks before they venture outside.

Front cover: Curled up, this young fawn waits patiently for its mother in the safety of Big Meadows.

Back cover: A raccoon kit peeks out of its nest in a tree snag.

ISBN 10: 1-56037-461-6
ISBN 13: 978-1-56037-461-9

© 2007 by Farcountry Press
Photography © 2007 by Ann and Rob Simpson
Text by Ann and Rob Simpson

For more information about our books, write Farcountry Press, P.O. Box 5630, Helena, MT 59604; call (800) 821-3874; or visit www.farcountrypress.com.

Created, produced, and designed in the United States.
Printed in China.

12 11 10 09 08 07   1 2 3 4 5 6

This eastern box turtle is sporting its specialized egg tooth, the hardened area on the tip of its nose that helps the baby turtle poke through its leathery egg. The tooth, or caruncle, will fall off several days after the turtle is hatched.

Introduction
by Ann and Rob Simpson

Our early summer pilgrimage to Shenandoah National Park is a tradition. Every June, we reserve rooms at the lodge, gather our equipment, and head out with our students into Big Meadows to photograph the year's fawns. Like so many of its animals, we make an annual migration to the park. As biologists, we are curious about wild animals. Our fascination with baby wild animals, however, goes beyond pure science. Whether it is the newness of a fawn or the playfulness of a bear cub, we believe nature is life's greatest instructor. And, in *Born Wild in Shenandoah*, we hope to share with you one of nature's most amazing creations: a baby wild animal.

Shenandoah National Park is home to numerous migratory birds. Every year they leave their southern homes and head north to take advantage of the huge flush of spring and summer protein: insects. Neotropical birds, including the wood thrush and yellow-billed cuckoo, make the yearly journey to find food, shelter, and a place to raise a family. Even seedeaters and hummingbirds feed their young this high-energy food to quickly fledge them out of the vulnerable nest.

In Shenandoah's lower elevations, spring arrives in February. The over-flights of common grackles and red-winged blackbirds signal the northward trek of migrating songbirds. The first litters of squirrel pups are born in nests of leaves in tall deciduous trees, such as oaks. In caves, black bear cubs nurse, helpless and dependent, on their mother's milk.

Spring is a series of changes. With spring, comes the sound of *fee-bee, fee-bee* as Eastern phoebes announce their arrival from more southerly climes, looking to nest on cliffs or under the eaves of park buildings. Eastern bluebirds look for cavities, such as abandoned woodpecker holes, to use as nesting sites. Spotted salamanders leave their underground nests and search for wetlands in which to lay their eggs. Opossums and raccoons roam the shadowy nights looking for mates. Our noses tell us it is the skunks' mating season; they leave a heady reminder of their nocturnal territorial disputes. To some, the nighttime serenade of chorus frogs accompanied by the staccato sounds of spring peepers heralds spring.

April's warming temperatures coax redbud trees to burst forth in a shower of pale pinks on a sea of green leaves in the park's lower elevations. Mourning cloak butterflies come out of hibernation to linger on sunny patches of bare ground waiting for mates. A tiny brown

Henry's elfin butterfly, which spent its winter as a chrysalis and emerged as a newly transformed adult in April, drinks nectar from a redbud flower.

At higher elevations, spring arrives a month later, as the temperatures are 10 to 12 degrees colder and the persistent wind is biting. In snug dens, bobcat kittens are born. Ruby-throated hummingbirds arrive just as columbine and trumpet honeysuckle begin to bloom. When midges and caddisflies hatch, birds including vireos, orioles, tanagers, and kingbirds make the scene. Twenty-four species of warblers return from their neotropical wintering grounds and waste no time in building nests, laying eggs and launching new generations.

Throughout the park, May is a transitional month. In early May, the lower elevations are lush with bright new foliage, but on the mountaintops, the tree buds are still tightly closed. While Carolina wrens are fledging young in the lowlands, the higher-elevation birds may just be building nests. By the end of the month, the park is in full bloom. The leaves are lush and waterfalls, swollen from the spring rains, thunder over rocks. A new generation of chipmunks scampers about the stone walls lining Skyline Drive. Appalachian juncos, which live in the park year-round, begin building their nests on high slopes and cliffs. Wild turkey hens and their flocks of eight to fifteen poults graze at the edge of the oak forests. From nests on Stony Man Mountain, newly fledged peregrine falcons take their first flights.

For wildlife enthusiasts, June is the most exciting month to visit Shenandoah. Does can be seen grazing in Big Meadows, often followed by gangly fawns. By late June, the fawns will have grown strong enough to venture out on their own and can be seen scampering about the meadow.

On hazy summer days, new animals learn to find food and shelter, while keeping constant watch for predators. Their hearing becomes more finely attuned. They now rely more on their speedy legs, rather than their camouflage colors, to protect them. Yet, even as summer wanes, babies are still being born. When the thistle down is on the fly, the American goldfinch starts nest-building. On the park's highest mountains, endangered Shenandoah salamanders are hatching from their eggs in moist nests.

In fall, the park's wildlife prepares for the winter ahead. Birds, that hatched just months ago, migrate to the tropics. Caterpillars wrap themselves tightly in cocoons to prepare for the coming winter. The fawns have started losing their spots. As their predecessors have done, young squirrels scamper about, busily gathering acorns to cache for winter. Juvenile bears ravenously eat their fill of berries to store up fat reserves for their long winter's sleep.

As the circle of life continues, we too think ahead to a new season in Shenandoah National Park. We sign up a new group of students. We make our lodge reservations. And we anticipate another Shenandoah spring sunrise, highlighting the soft coats of Big Meadows fawns.

According to folk tales, if woolly bear caterpillars sport relatively narrow orange bands, it will be a harsh winter. A wider band means that a milder winter is coming. These familiar caterpillars are the larval form of the Isabella tiger moth.

Above: This cowbird squats on the nest of a solitary vireo. Cowbirds do not build their own nests; instead they take over the nests of other birds. Cowbirds lay their eggs in the nest, and the host birds, such as these vireos, feed the chicks as if they were their own.

Facing page: Foxes are common in the park's lower elevations and in Shenandoah Valley. In March and April, vixens bear litters of five pups that stay in the den for about five weeks. The female nurses the pups for more than two months, and the male supplements the diet by bringing them insects and mice.

Above: An immature peregrine falcon takes a sidelong glance. In Shenandoah's tallest mountains, the sharp calls of *kee-kee-kee* are testimony to the success of the peregrine falcon reintroduction effort in the East. From 1950 to 1970, DDT poisoning caused a thinning of the birds' eggshells, and the peregrine's population crashed. After a vigorous reintroduction effort, the peregrine falcon was removed from the endangered species list in 1999.

Left: The only marsupials north of Mexico, Virginia opossums, or "possums," live on a wide variety of foodstuffs, including spoiled food. Seven to nine joeys are born at a time and claw their way to their mother's pouch, where they remain for several months. After they are weaned, the babies are carried about on their mother's back.

Facing page: The five-lined skink, or blue-tailed skink, is a reptile that has scales and not the glandular skin of amphibians. The bright blue tail of the baby gradually fades to a dull gray as the skink ages. Skinks can be found most often on rocky ridges and valley shale barrens.

Above: Looking somewhat like an alien, the silver-spotted skipper caterpillar has bright-yellow eyespots that help frighten away predators. If further provoked, it stretches out its wrinkled, red neck like a miniature snake. This uniquely decorated caterpillar feeds at night and hides during the day by covering itself with a folded black locust leaf.

Right: A white-tailed fawn scampers in Big Meadows, exercising its growing legs. Deer rely on their ability to run and jump quickly to escape predators. An adult whitetail can run as fast as 35 miles per hour and can clear a 12-foot fence.

Left: These three eastern gray squirrels were born, blind and hairless, in late February. Their eyes will not open until they are five weeks old, but at two months old, they will not require their mother's care.

Facing page: Unlike their red-breasted parents, American robin chicks are spotted, which helps camouflage the chicks when they leave the nest and are not yet skilled fliers. Two-week-old robin chicks hop out of the nest onto the ground, where they remain while their parents continue to bring them food.

Below: This young black rat snake emerges from its egg, most likely in late summer. Unlike its black parents, the hatchling is highly patterned with splotches, which gives rise to the local legend that black rat snakes breed with copperheads.

Above: Four deer mice curl in a nest. Although deer mice are the most widespread rodent in North American, they live primarily in elevations above 3,000 feet in Shenandoah. They look similar to the more common white-footed mouse but have a longer white-tipped tail.

Left: A raccoon kit perches precariously on a snag. In May, litters of three to four raccoon kits are born in hollow trees. Their mother nurses the kits for three months, then the kits begin to venture out with her for food. Primarily nocturnal, raccoons are omnivores and eat a variety of plants, insects, and small mammals. Park visitors must not feed the raccoons or allow them to vandalize their campsites.

Above: This Shenandoah salamander is found only in the park's higher elevations—and nowhere else in the world. Listed on the federal endangered species list, this salamander comes in two colors: black with a bit of white around the face or black with a red stripe down its back. Since they have no lungs, these salamanders absorb oxygen directly through their moist glandular skin.

Right: This black bear pauses, mid-step, in the middle of a meadow. Black bear cubs are born in January, when the sows are snuggled in their dens. Weighing only seven to fifteen ounces at birth, a black bear cub is 1/250 the weight of the mother. Black bears are often seen near the Big Meadows and Skyland areas and occasionally along Skyline Drive at dusk.

Above: The brilliantly colored azalea caterpillar that feeds on azalea and maleberry bushes turns into the dull-colored major datana moth. In late summer, hikers frequently see these large yellow-and-black-splotched caterpillars with red legs and a red head munching on the leaves of low bushes in Big Meadows.

Right: A meadow vole is tucked in its nest of grass. One of the most prolific mammals in North America, meadow vole females give birth to six or seven young as many as seventeen times during the breeding season and produce as many as one hundred babies in one year!

Facing page: Four downy red-shouldered hawk eyas nest in a deciduous tree. Although red-shouldered hawks prefer riparian areas and wooded swamps, the adult and young hawks fly over the meadows to hunt. Unlike some hawks, which are relatively secretive around their nests, the red-shouldered hawk is noisy and displays aerial acrobatics.

Below: With its long whiskers and shiny nose, the northern short-tailed shrew is a secretive mammal that lives in tunnels. They breed in spring and summer, producing litters of four to seven honeybee-sized babies, but few live longer than a year. The shrew's saliva contains venom that paralyzes its prey, which includes insects and mice.

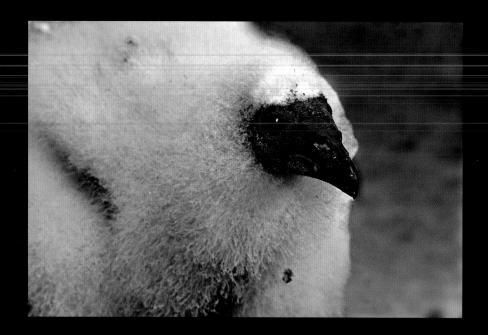

Above: Covered in white down, this turkey vulture chick's black head will become bald and red as it ages. Occasionally called mountain eagles, turkey vultures are erroneously known as buzzards and are actually related to storks. From Stony Man Overlook, they can be seen soaring on the cliff-side air currents. An area bird count recently recorded the highest number of turkey vultures in North America.

Right: A coyote pup sits primly on the forest floor. A recent arrival from the West, coyotes have found their way to Shenandoah, where their well-known *yip-yip-yoweee* calls are occasionally heard. One of North America's most successful carnivore species, coyotes form pairs that can last for years, and both parents care for the pups by bringing them food such as mice and insects.

Above: Found in the park's cool mountain streams, brook trout young have vertical lines on their sides known as par marks that help to camouflage the fry when they are small. In late October, brook trout spawn in the gravelly riffles of Shenandoah's streams.

Facing page: Poised in a sea of green, this sturdy woodchuck—also known as a whistle-pig or groundhog—lives on the edge of the park's forests. In April or May, litters of two to seven young are born in burrows. Over the winter, woodchucks hibernate in their burrows by decreasing their heartbeats from seventy-five to four beats per minute.

Above: The eye of this immature male northern cardinal is colored a dull brown. As the bird matures, the iris color will deepen to a dark brown. The bird has started molting its bright red feathers, but it will not be fully red until next spring. The bill color will change to bright orange.

Left: The state bird of Virginia, the northern cardinal is common in the park's lower elevations. Both male and female cardinals care for the young, bringing the chicks treats such as caterpillars and other insects.

Above: Throughout the park, brightly striped monarch butterfly caterpillars can be found wherever milkweed plants grow. The caterpillars eat the milkweed leaves and acquire the poisonous latex of the plant. This helps the adult monarch protect itself from predators because, after one taste, predators, such as hungry birds, will spit out the caterpillar.

Facing page: The Appalachian azure butterfly only lays its eggs on black cohosh plants. If you look closely, you can see the tiny white eggs on the flower buds and stalks. When the larvae hatch, they will eat the flowers of the black cohosh.

Right: A cluster of baby orb weaver spiders clings to a wild geranium. Spiders lay their eggs in a protected sac of silk. When the spiderlings hatch out, they congregate together before dispersing, often cannibalizing one another, then they climb to a high spot on a branch, release strands of silk, and float off to a new life.

Following pages: Wood ducklings walk single file through the forest. The only duck that nests in the park, the wood duck nests high in the cavities of deciduous trees, such as sycamores. The ducklings are born with sharp toes and can climb out of the nest cavity and jump down as far as sixty-five feet.

29

Above: Called a polecat by mountain people, a striped skunk pores over the ground, looking for a beetle grub. The word skunk is actually derived from the Algonquin Indian word *seganku*, meaning "one who squirts." Skunk kits are born in April or May, blind and fully dependent on their mother's milk. Their scent glands are fully functional when they are two weeks old.

Right: This black rat snake curls around a clutch of its eggs. Black rat snakes earn their name by eating rodents, such as rats and mice, and local farmers encourage the snakes to live in their barns and outbuildings to keep the rodent populations at bay. A common folk tale suggests that in times of danger, black snakes lead rattlesnakes to safety—hence the nickname, pilot snakes.

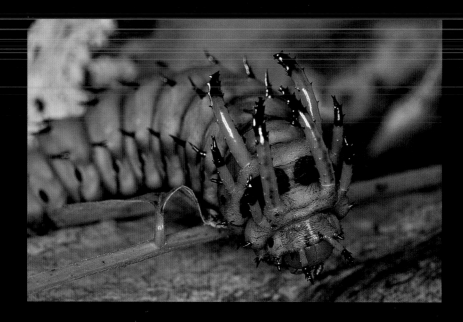

Above: This ferocious-looking hickory-horned devil caterpillar is the larva of the beautiful pink and yellow royal walnut moth. Although it appears dangerous, the caterpillar is harmless.

Facing page: Perched sideways on a twig, this cerulean warbler was born in the park, but will migrate to South America for the winter. Cerulean warblers nest high in mature deciduous trees, but as the forest habitats have disappeared, their numbers have declined. Refuges like Shenandoah provide critical breeding areas for this sensitive neotropical species.

Above: A female southern flying squirrel curls around its dozing pups. Born in tree cavities or old woodpecker holes, the pups are blind and hairless and nurse for two months. A southern flying squirrel does not actually fly but sails by spreading out the membranous flap between its front and hind legs.

Facing page: Round and fragile, these sparrow eggs wait in a cup-shaped nest. Song sparrows prefer habitats such as park overlooks, scrublands, or meadows; the speckled coloration helps camouflage the eggs. Birds that lay eggs in cup-shaped nests often have round eggs, whereas eggs laid on cliffs are often oval-shaped.

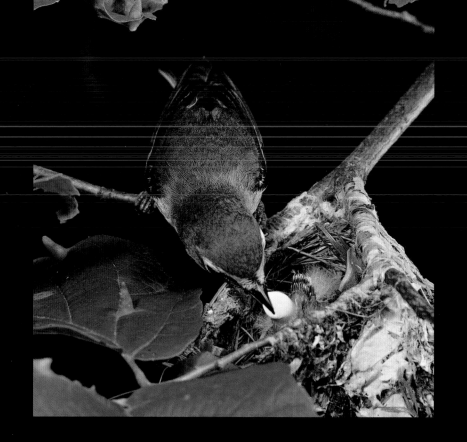

Above: This solitary vireo cleans out its nest by picking up the chicks' special enclosed fecal sacs and disposing of them far from the nest. This prevents nest contamination, which could attract predators or disease. When the chicks begin flying, they no longer produce these specialized waste sacs.

Left: Dented, white, and opaque, these are pipevine swallowtail butterfly eggs. When they hatch, the larvae feed on Virginia Snakeroot and Dutchman's Pipe, which makes the larvae and butterfly toxic to predators.

Facing page: With its brown cap, and black eyes and nose, this white-tailed fawn is a partial albino. True albinos have pure white fur and pink eyes. One partial albino doe the locals have dubbed "Dolly" has become famous around the Skyland Resort area. Some of her offspring have normal coloration, and others are partially white.

Above: During its spawning season in May, female smallmouth bass lay up to 2,000 eggs. The eggs hatch in about five days, and the male guards the fry for about two weeks until they disperse to make it on their own.

Facing page: This smooth green snake, also called the green grass snake, can be found in high-elevation grassy areas, such as Big Meadows and Old Rag Overlook. The female snake lays three to twelve eggs in June and July and the hatchlings emerge in early fall.

Right: A sweet symbiosis: Allegheny mound builder ants milk insects, such as this treehopper, for a sugary by-product called honeydew and, in return, the ants defend the treehoppers from predators. The ants' mounds—two feet tall and cone-shaped—can be seen near Gooney Manor Overlook.

Right: Nose twitching, this eastern cottontail is a common sight in the park's open areas. In dense thickets or hollow logs, does produce litters of three to six bunnies a year. Bunnies leave the nest and begin to forage when they are two weeks old, eating grass and wild strawberries in summer, twigs and bark in winter.

Facing page: This gray fox stops, ears cocked, listening. Gray foxes den in hollow logs or ground burrows and in April or May, females give birth to litters of three or four pups. With their distinctive salt-and-pepper coat and black-tipped tail, the nocturnal gray fox is rarely seen, even though it is fairly common at the park's lower elevations.

Below: This fuzzy American kestrel chick cocks its head. These small falcons can be seen near the park's boundaries, hovering in midair, scouring the Shenandoah Valley's fields and farmlands for prey. American kestrels prefer to breed in open areas, such as those near Beagle Gap.

Above: Looking a bit like a punk rock star, this common grackle chick has fluffy down feathers in its juvenile plumage. In mid-February, common grackles return to Virginia from wintering in the southern United States. At the park's periphery, they set up territories and begin to nest.

Right: Odd-looking gypsy moth larvae, such as this one, were responsible for killing millions of trees in Shenandoah. Gypsy moths eat oak leaves, the park's predominant tree species. This insect was introduced to the United States by someone who hoped to start a silkworm business. Not one yard of silk was produced, but the insect has defoliated millions of trees.

Facing page: The Appalachian species of slate-colored juncos are Shenandoah's "snow birds." A year-round park resident, the slate-colored junco breeds on high-altitude slopes and cliffs, although it may move to lower elevations when the temperatures drop.

Above: This solitary vireo rests easy in its intricately woven nest.
Skillful nest builders, solitary vireos often weave lichens, shredded
bark, spider webs, and insect cocoons into their nests. Cowbirds
will try to lay their eggs in the nests, but the vireos often respond
by building a second nest floor over the cowbird egg.

Facing page: A black bear cub rolls on its back, paws up. Black bears
are intelligent and curious. They have excellent memories and
navigational skills and young bears can find food sources that their
mothers showed them years before. Black bears eat plants, berries,
and nuts; this high-carbohydrate diet lacks fat and protein, so bears
will often seek these out in the food and garbage people leave
behind. Park picnickers and campers must safely store their food
and never feed the animals, because once bears become a nuisance,
they often have to be killed.

Above: A spotted salamander larva takes a tentative step. During the first warm, moist evenings of early spring, spotted salamanders emerge from their subterranean tunnels and head for ancestral breeding pools, choosing temporary ponds that fill with waters from spring thaws but soon dry up. There is a reason for this: the short-lived pools do not contain fish that would devour the salamander eggs. Spotted salamanders are uncommon in the park, but can be found in Big Meadows.

Facing page: Half-mast and open: one downy screech owl dozes while another waits for its mother to return with a meal. Common at the lower and middle elevations in the park, screech owls are cavity nesters. Females give birth in May to four or five owlets, and all three color morphs—brown, red, and gray—may be found in the same nest.

Above: Its colors may be brilliant, but this spiny oak slug caterpillar has venomous spines. If a predator or curious human happens to touch a spiny oak caterpillar, they will receive a sting similar to that of a honeybee. These intriguing caterpillars turn into dull brown spiny oak slug moths.

Right: This immature ruby-throated male hummingbird drinks nectar from a flowering jewelweed. Ruby-throated hummingbirds are the only hummingbirds commonly found in Virginia. Males are smaller than females, and immature males can often be identified in late summer by a single red feather on their throats.

Facing page: The wide mouths of field sparrow chicks herald spring from a nest deep in a Tartarian honeysuckle. Male field sparrows return annually to their home breeding grounds and their trilling calls announce their arrival. Females prefer to find new nests. Field sparrows prefer open areas such as those in Big Meadows.

Below: This red eft is the final larval stage of the red-spotted newt. Unlike most salamanders, which have pollywog-like aquatic larvae, red-spotted newts have a larval stage that is terrestrial. Unlike other salamanders, the red eft larvae are able to walk around in broad daylight because their granular skin helps prevent dehydration. They also have the most toxic skin glands of any North American animal.

Above: One of the most common rodents in the forest, the white-footed mouse is also one of the most common prey species. The female gives birth to four to six young several times a year. Like all mammals, the female provides nourishing milk during the early stages of the babies' development.

Right: North America's largest rodent, beavers use their chisel-like teeth to construct dams and lodges. Their front teeth are highly specialized for gnawing through wood, and the enamel of their large incisors contains iron for extra strength, hence the orange color. Nearly extinct in the early 1900s, beavers have been successfully reintroduced and can be seen in the park at Rapidan Camp, Skyland, South River Falls, Big Run, and Milam Gap.

Above: This bright prairie warbler hails not from the prairie, as its name implies, but was originally named for a barren area in Kentucky. Prairie warblers spend the winter in Florida and then migrate back to Virginia in spring. After the two to five warbler chicks hatch, the mother quickly eats the discarded eggshells, which provides her with calcium. In Shenandoah, these warblers nest in the park's lower elevations.

Facing page: Fierce, this young golden-eyed, sharp-shinned hawk scans a field for prey. The age of a "sharp-shin" can be determined by certain characteristics. An immature sharp-shinned hawk, like this one, has a yellow iris; adults have red irises. Young birds also have vertical brown chest stripes, as opposed to the horizontal bars found on adults.

Above: During spring and summer, the flute-like song of the wood thrush serenades hikers along Shenandoah's forested trails. Because its numbers are declining, the migratory wood thrush has become the "poster bird" of conservationist efforts to save the rainforest. Wood thrush nests are often in hemlock trees, which now face a new threat: the hemlock woolly adelgid that has killed the giant stands of hemlock trees in Shenandoah.

Right: A young white-tailed fawn nuzzles the delicate fuzz of a dandelion, satisfying its curiosity about its surroundings. Deer have acute senses of hearing, smell, and sight—although they are color-blind—that they use to detect danger. In fall, the fawns lose their white spots and their gray-brown winter coat molts in to protect them from the winter cold.

Facing page: This mottled sculpin lives in clear, fast-flowing mountain streams, as do the brook trout that dine on the sculpin fingerlings. Sculpins have an interesting mating ritual. The male sculpin entices the female sculpin into a rocky cave. After the female deposits her gooey eggs onto the cave's ceiling, the male fertilizes them and then stands guard, fanning the eggs with his huge pectoral fins to keep them oxygenated and silt-free.

Below: Ruffed grouse camouflage their dun-colored chicks in earthen colored leaves. If danger persists, the female gathers all of her young under her.

Above: The aptly named saddleback caterpillar inflicts a painful sting with the sharp bristles on its body. The distinctively marked larva feeds on a wide variety of herbaceous plants.

Right: This least shrew pokes its head out of its nest of grass. Only three inches long, the least shrew females bear two to seven young, each less than an inch long. The babies eat insects and worms constantly because, with a heartbeat of more than 1,000 beats per minute and an exceedingly high metabolic rate, they may die if they miss a meal.

Left: Splayed against the trunk of an oak tree, this little brown bat baby, or pup, is one of nature's true flying mammals. It navigates the night skies, devouring as many as 1,200 insects an hour. In mid-June after hibernating all winter, female little brown bats congregate in nursery colonies and bear single, hairless pups.
PHOTO BY BILL BEATTY

Below: At dawn and dusk, wild turkey hens and their flocks of eight to fifteen baby turkeys, called poults, graze at the edge of the park's forest. Poults can forage on their own twenty-four hours after they hatch.

Facing page: A pileated woodpecker feeds a nest full of hungry chicks. Year-round residents of Shenandoah, these striking, red-crested birds can be heard drumming their bills on tree trunks throughout the park. Pileated woodpeckers bore large cavities into trees for nests that often face toward the south or east to catch the sun.

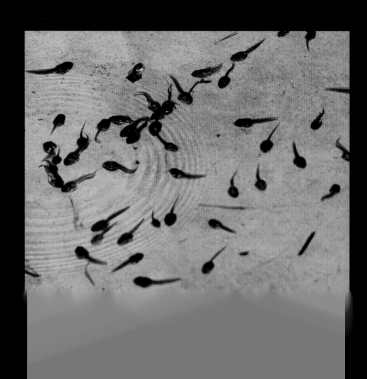

Above: Curled into their nest of dried grasses, willow flycatcher chicks are fragile and eerie-looking. Willow flycatchers are found in the swampy areas of Big Meadows, where they nest in low shrubby vegetation.

Right: This army of wood frog tadpoles swarms about the ephemeral pools that collect in Big Meadows Campground. The tadpoles will metamorphose into the adult wood frogs that, during their springtime courtship rituals, make quacking, duck-like calls.

Far right: A white-tailed doe and her fawn graze peacefully along a well-worn trail through Big Meadows.

Facing page: This bobcat kitten looks intently into the woods. Nocturnal animals, bobcats are common in Shenandoah but are only occasionally seen perched on the stone walls along Skyline Drive. Mountain people recognize the bobcat's eerie call, which sounds like a baby's scream and has been likened to the banshee's scream, the ancient Irish spirit forewarning death.

Below: Born helpless and naked in a grass nest, this southern red-backed vole will be fully mature by three months. In Shenandoah, southern red-backed voles produce two to three litters of babies annually. A favorite food of bobcats, foxes, and owls, the vole's life span in the wild is less than one year.

Right: Found in areas of dry quartzite in the park's southern district, the hognose snake hatchling will puff up its body before it has fully emerged from its egg, flatten its head like a cobra, and make an ominous hissing noise, looking a bit like poisonous pit viper. As this snake is not poisonous, this is a bluff.

Facing page: The adult cedar waxwing has the red waxy substance on its wing tip. The immature bird will acquire this later. Cedar waxwings are one of the last birds to nest in Shenandoah; their reproduction coincides with the ripening of fruit that makes up most of their diet.

Below: Probably the most common snake in Shenandoah National Park, this juvenile ringneck snake looks similar to the adult but has a dull-colored back and black head. According to legend, ringneck snakes are young eastern kingsnakes, and they continue to add rings until they are grown. A ringneck snake is only about a foot long, whereas the adult eastern kingsnake can be more than four feet.

Above: Look closely and the pink gape on the hinge of this common raven's bill identifies it as a hatchling. Throughout the park, the raucous *rronk-rronk* calls of common ravens can be heard as they fly from high-altitude perches such as Stony Man and Old Rag Mountain. Born in nests on cliffs, the chicks grow up to be the largest songbirds in the world.

Right: A northern dusky salamander shines against the wet rocks. Unlike many types of salamanders that lay eggs and leave them, northern dusky salamanders lay their clutch of eggs in a moist area under a rock, and then the female stays with the eggs as they develop. Look closely to see the tiny young salamanders developing in these eggs.

Above: A Louisiana waterthrush female busily feeds three hungry chicks. One of the first neotropical migrants to return to Shenandoah each spring, the Louisiana waterthrush is categorized as a warbler, although its appearance suggests that of a thrush or sparrow. When the males return to the park in spring they energetically sing, and their loud ringing calls can be heard for long distances over the rushing mountain streams.

Right: Nestled in a meadow, twin fawns scamper about this white-tailed doe. In their first breeding season, does usually only have one fawn, but in subsequent years they often bear twins. During the first month, the mother hides the newborn fawns while she forages, returning to nurse them three or four times a day.

Above: Standing guard over her eggs, this female Acadian flycatcher is one of three species of flycatchers that breed in Shenandoah. The Acadian flycatcher breeds in low-elevation forests and along waterways such as South River Falls.

Right: This young broad-winged hawk is silhouetted as it sits on its nest in a beech tree. In fall, large numbers or "kettles" of hawks can be seen from park overlooks, such as Stony Man, Hogback and Gooney Run, as they begin their migration from Shenandoah to South America. In the spring, the broad-winged hawks nest in the park, raising broods of two to three young.

Above: A great horned owlet stares intently, its yellow eyes ablaze. Great horned owls often take over other birds' nests to lay a clutch of two to three eggs in the chilly month of January. The owlets fledge when they are two-and-a-half months old, but before they are ready for sustained flight, they occasionally can be found on the ground, where the parents continue to feed them.

Right: Its wings akimbo, this young male American redstart has yellow and black plumage, in contrast to the orange and black coloring of the adult male. When they return from their wintering grounds in May, American redstarts are one of the most numerous breeding bird species in Shenandoah National Park.

Rob Simpson is a professor of natural resources and the head of the nature and outdoor photography program at Lord Fairfax Community College in Virginia, teaching courses in field biology and nature photography. Born in Canada, Rob has worked as a park naturalist in Ontario's Rondeau Provincial Park, as an environmental inventory scientist locating rare and endangered plants and animals for the Department of Natural Resources, and as a field research scientist for the Canadian Wildlife Service. He has discovered two new plant taxa, which were named after him—*Spiranthes x simpsonii* and *Dryosticum x simpsonii.*

    Ann Simpson is a professor of anatomy and physiology, and chairs the science department at Lord Fairfax Community College. She co-teaches nature photography classes with Rob and organizes the international nature photography and natural history tours that she and Rob lead to countries including Africa, Canada, Costa Rica, Ecuador, the Galapagos Islands, Trinidad, and Tobago.

    The Simpsons' expertise as professional biologists gives their photography an in-depth style. As owners of Simpsons' Nature Photography, they specialize in photographing rare species. With Farcountry Press, they have published *Born Wild in the Smokies* and *Shenandoah National Park Simply Beautiful.* Their images have appeared in publications including *National Geographic, National Parks, National Geographic KIDS,* and in *American Park Network Guides,* and *Birds of Shenandoah National Park.* Recently, the Simpsons were chosen to lead photography seminars for Canon and American Park Network. Their work can be seen at www.agpix.com/snphotos.